Table of Contents

Cybersecurity Jobs:
Resume Marketing
Book 1
Find Cybersecurity Jobs

By

Bruce Brown, CISSP, ISC2 CAP

www.convocourses.com[1]

contact@convocourses.com

1. *http://www.convocourses.com*

Download free ATS resume templates at:

convocourses.com/courses/resume[2]

Check us out on:

youtube.com/convocourses

Contact us:

contact@convocourses.com

2. http://convocourses.com/courses/resume

Expected Results

I get nonstop job offers on my phone, via email and through direct messages. It actually gets annoying. But this is what you want ... options.

I receive offers with a variety of salaries, locations, and types of positions with all kinds of benefits and even short-term contracts that pay high but have no benefits. I have so many options that I am evaluating each employer and it's no big deal if I decide not to take that position or if they select someone else because I have so many other opportunities.

I have all these options because I know how to market a solid resume. I create searchable resumes for the jobs I am most qualified; then I post them on a lot of job sites.

These days all the tools that we need are there; we just need to know how to implement them.

To be honest, 90 percent of the jobs are not for me. There are a few reasons for this. It might be that the job is not even in my profession or it is in my profession but I'm not qualified for the position or sometimes I just don't want the position. I would say about 3 percent of the positions that are sent to me are something that would pay me well and I would be OK with the work.

I am OK with that 3 percent because the more I apply for, the better my chances of getting something I really want. And I could always settle for something in the 10 percent range. Those are usually the jobs with a long commute, or require me to move, or do some travel. Even the more uncomfortable options are a huge blessing. I am not worried during recessions, or if oil and gas prices are crazy.

No matter what, I am OK and my family is OK because I can find work or create work. That is the power of marketing yourself.

This book will walk you through how I have been able to get these kinds of results.

Obviously, everyone's results will vary. We all have different levels of experience, skill sets and qualifications, but by the end of this process you will have a method of opening more doors than ever before.

In this book we will focus mostly on cybersecurity jobs—but the techniques can be used in just about any profession, not just cybersecurity and information technology. If you are in health care, banking, retail, sanitation or any job that requires a resume, these methods can help you because ultimately, they are about marketing yourself effectively using your resume.

Steps to Take Action!

In order to have success and expanded opportunities, we need to go through the process of creating and positioning a resume that employers want. This book will help you create that resume.

We will use these steps:

- **Get tools** – There are basic things we need to have before we start.
- **ATS format** – In this section we go into detail about the application tracking software and the resume format that is necessary.
- **Work experience** – We will put the keywords together to show your cybersecurity experience and explore what is needed.
- **Degrees** – What degrees are needed for cybersecurity?
- **Certification** – Certain categories of cybersecurity prefer certain certifications.
- **Skills** – The skills section is a great opportunity to put in keywords.
- **Career paths** – Before we gather keywords, we need to know the direction you want to go with your career.
- **Find keywords** – This is research into what will be needed on your resume to make it more attractive.
- **Create a profile** – Before we market the resume, we need to create a profile.
- **Market the resume** – Where do you post your resume? How do you market yourself?
- **Appendix A:** entry-level certs – If you have little or no experience, you can check out these entry-level IT certifications to get an idea of where to start.

Tools You Will Need

There are some tools that will make this process much easier to do. In order to create our resume, we will start with software that can give us a blank page.

You can use a blank document on a word processor. Any of these will do:

- Microsoft Word
- Google Docs
- Open Office
- Apple Pages
- Notepad
- WordPad

Any of these will do. This document will not have any graphics, tables or fancy formatting.

The easiest thing to do is use one of my free templates at:

convocoures.com/courses/resume[1]

We will be building your resume in a simple .doc or .docx in an arrangement that is acceptable to application tracking systems.

1. http://convocourses.com/courses/resume

Set up marketing

How we set up marketing for the resume will depend on the industry you are trying to get into and the country you live in. This book focuses on cybersecurity and IT roles but the technique can work in just about any profession.

Let's start with countries. If you are in the United States or wanting to find a job in the USA, you will need accounts on the following sites:

- LinkedIn
- Dice.com
- Monster.com
- Ziprecruiter
- CareerBuilder
- Indeed.com
- Glassdoor
- AngelList
- PostJobFree
- Startupers
- Jobxoom
- Job Spider
- ReliefWeb
- Jobvertise

This list of job sites is ever changing so always do your own research. You just need the current list of top job sites in the country you want to work from.

Set up marketing for any country

No matter what country you are in or want to work from, you can market yourself there. There is no guarantee that you can get work there, but it doesn't hurt to try.

Each country has a different set of job sites that works better there so we need to find that top 10. To find them, go to your favorite search engine and type: "Top 10 job sites [country]."

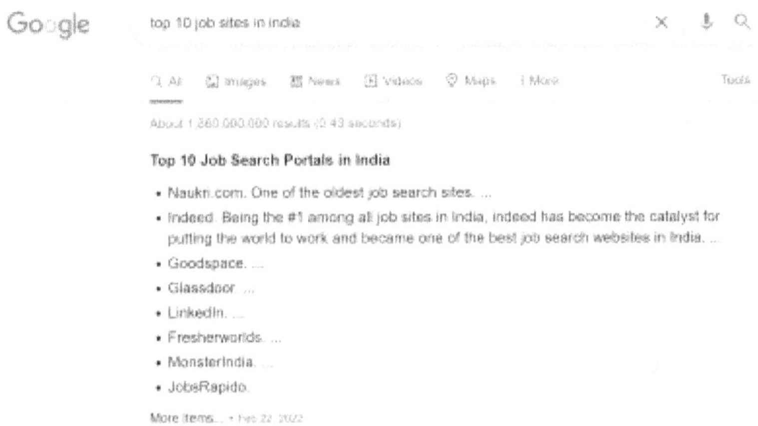

In this case we searched for "Top 10 job sites in India." Our results as of this writing are the following:

- Naukri.com
- Indeed
- Goodspace
- Glassdoor
- LinkedIn
- Fresherworlds
- MonsterIndia
- JobsRapido
- Upwork
- Shine

A few pointers about this search. Avoid the paid ad links. Go to the top organic results. Also, compare your list against at least two other top lists. You will find job sites that pop up among the top of the same lists. These are your first priority.

Another alternative is to look for remote jobs in multiple countries and work from whatever country you want.

What Is ATS?

The resume we will build will be arranged to be acceptable to application tracking systems (ATS). An ATS is software that most recruiters and employers use to track candidates as they go through the recruiting process.

An ATS-style resume is very simple with sections labeled a certain way, with no fancy-looking formats or fonts. The sections and labels we will address in separate chapters. The recommended fonts are Times New Roman, Calibri, Arial, or Georgia.

Organizations (corporate or government) ATS systems can be built into a database that allows them to collect and sort through hundreds of resumes they have collected or it can be a full suite of tools that make it possible to analyze all potential candidates.

An application tracking system helps the organization do the following:

Make the onboarding process faster

With a specific format that has all of the data they need from each candidate, the employer can make sure they have everything they need to start work.

Be competitive

Most of the top 500 largest companies in the United States (Fortune 500 companies) use an ATS system because it makes the hiring process easier. Each of these companies is competing to get the best and brightest hired as quicky as possible before their competition gets them.

More efficient and cheaper

With a streamlined method of collecting information from potential candidates, the organization can give fewer tasks to their recruiters. This tool helps them sort through more resumes faster.

Find qualified candidates faster

With standardized data collected from the ATS resume, the organization can use artificial intelligence and machine learning to identify skills and predict success factors that help them find the best fit.

The bottom line is that the ATS resume makes it easier for the employer to find you and hire you.

How ATS works

The application tracking system processes each resume by breaking it into sections. These sections are important to cybersecurity:

- Work Experience
- Education
- Skills
- Languages
- Certifications

There are other sections that ATS can read but these are the most essential that we will stick to in this book.

ATS searches for keywords, key phrases and qualifications to see if your resume matches the job description.

Here is an example of how ATS sees your cybersecurity resume:

"Motivated expert with 3 years of experience in cybersecurity. Extensive troubleshooting on TCP/IP networking issues. Proven track record of success, employer satisfaction, and strong communication skills. Security clearance: secret."

ATS sees:

"Cybersecurity"
"3 years of experience"
"TCP/IP"
"Networking"
"Strong communication skills"
"Security clearance"

Then, ATS matches what it gathers from your resume to the organizations list of requirements:

Cybersecurity [CHECK]
3 years of experience [CHECK]
TCP/IP [CHECK]

Communication skills [CHECK]
CCNA [missing]
Microsoft Office [missing]

This is just an example of things that might be checked based on the ATS assessing your resume keywords, key phrases and qualifications against a job's requirements. If your resume doesn't match the requirements, ATS will rate your resume accordingly and move on to the next.

Avoid the following items on your resume:

- Text boxes
- Logos
- Images
- Headers/footers
- Tables
- Hyperlinks
- Uncommon fonts (stick with Cambria, Times New Roman, Georgia, Arial, Helvetica, Garamond)

Popular ATS systems

If you have ever uploaded your resume or filled out an online job application in the past 5 years, there is a good chance you have used one of the more popular ATS systems. These include:

Taleo by Oracle. This system goes back to the 1990s. This system owns something like 20 percent of the market share for ATS systems and 30 percent of the Fortune 500. Corporations like Starbucks, Nike, Deloitte and Tesla have used Taleo.

iCIMS. I see iCIMS a lot on government contracting companies. It has about 7 percent of the ATS market share and has been used by Amazon, Samsung and Uber. Candidates are sorted based on the percentage of keyword matches and the same keyword can be used multiple times.

Greenhouse. This ATS is being used by Major League Baseball, Roku and Taco Bell. They go by keyword frequency. At the time of this writing, they have about 8 percent of the ATS market.

Other ATS systems you may have heard of include Jobvite, BrassRing, Workday, SAP, CareerBuilder and there are many others. About 8 percent of companies have their own proprietary ATS system.

What they all have in common is their focus on the sections and keywords to match job requirements. So, what you need to know is what job you are targeting (career path), what keywords to put in for that target job and what sections you need on your ATS resume. There are the things we will focus on in this book.

ATS Resume Format and Sections

The first thing you will notice about the ATS-style resume is that it is simple. It does not have fancy graphic overlays or comprehensive tables that break down all the skills and certifications. In fact, these things disrupt the ATS system so we must avoid this at all costs. The final files will be a .doc, .docx or .txt. We can also make it a PDF, but some older ATS systems cannot process PDFs so I would avoid this.

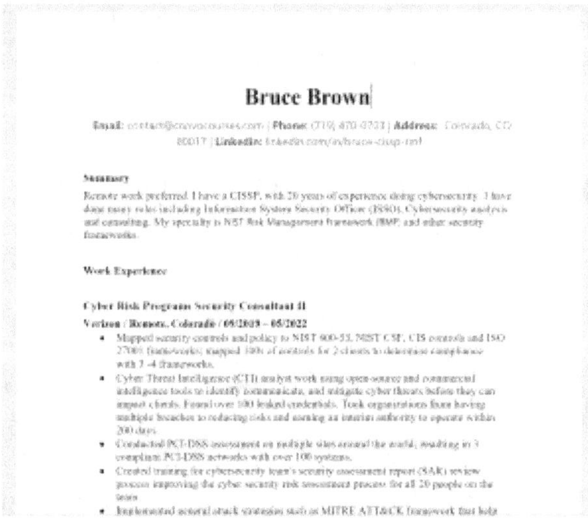

Basic ATS Resume

We need to have simple headers. Do not get creative with the headers in the resume.

Instead of saying something like "Where I have worked" as a header, we will keep it to "Work Experience." Instead of "My Skills," we will just say "Skills." For the sake of the ATS that the resume will get plugged into, we need to keep it plain and take the guesswork out of the equation. ATS knows what "Skills" means; however, it might not be able to parse "MY SKILLS" or "Professional Skills."

We will show the best format for each section of the ATS resume.

Your resume should be focused on one role and get straight to the point. For example, if you are trying to get a role in management, network administration or cloud computing then you need a resume that focuses on each one of these. The management resume should focus on your management skills and experience; your cloud computing should focus on cloud certifications, cloud skills and cloud experience. And the same goes for the network administration role.

If I go all the way back to the beginning of my career, I was actually a security guard in the air force. I won't include this on my resume for a security operations center (SOC) analyst position because the skills set for a SOC analyst has almost nothing to do with the skills I required as a security guard. But I might include the security guard experience on my resume to get a security control assessor (SCA) role because some SCAs conduct physical assessments just like security guards do. There is actual overlap in the experience skill sets and even certifications.

Mention your personal details & contact information

The resume should start with your name and contact information.

Bruce Brown

Email: contact@convocourses.com | **Phone:** (719) 470-0703 | **Address:** Colorado, CO 80017 | **Linkedin:** linkedin.com/in/bruce-cissp-mf

Now, what you have to remember is that your name and contact information will be publicly available. What I do is use an alias. I use my middle name and a different last name. It's too easy for someone to use my real name and figure out things I don't want them to know.

For more details on protecting your privacy, see the chapter on profiles.

Example of an ATS-friendly resume

Here is an example of a cybersecurity resume with the ATS template:

Brian Noble

Summary

IT & cybersecurity specialist with a secret security clearance eligibility and 2 years of experience in IT & cybersecurity at a medium-sized company. Well-developed skills implementing security controls and ensuring that servers and end-user devices (Windows and MAC) are configured securely.

506-124-6898 – BriNobes554@outlook.com – Fayetteville, North Carolina, 28303

Education

Associate Degree – Information Technology – Fayetteville Community College – 2019

- Working on BS in CS
- Extensive training using digital spreadsheets and formulas efficiently
- Earned a certificate in Security+ lab

Certifications

CompTIA Security + Certification

Project Management Professional Certification (PMP)

Work Experience

Help Desk Support – TirePlanet – April 2021–April 2022

- Troubleshooting end-users' laptops with network and software issues; support 150 users with multiple devices
- Managed Android and iPhone ensuring all company-owned mobile devices are tracked and data is encrypted
- Enabled audit logs on 34 mission-essential systems and 100 end-user laptops to conduct continuous monitoring and detect possible security incidents
- Created an incident response plan for all business essential servers supporting the southwest sites; virtual servers include Windows 2019 and RedHat systems

IT Customer Service – Ants – New Mexico – January 2020–December 2021

- Conducted quarterly risk assessment on over 200 business critical systems; created risk reports for the CIO and upper management
- Assisted the server team in installing 12 Windows 2019 servers migrating legacy systems to a new operating system
- Provided remote technical support for the workstations of over 1,500 customers; patient with difficult customers

Skills

- Programming language: C+, HTML, Fortran, COBOL
- Security clearance: Secret, TS/SCI, Public Trust

We will go into each section of the cybersecurity ATS resume so that we can increase the chances of getting more opportunities in this lucrative career path.

Summary Section

Label this section as "Summary" or "Objectives." I use "Summary" because it is more flexible. An Objective is a goal or thing aimed at, but a summary can be an introduction to your best skills and it can include goals if you want.

This section is a great opportunity to put in more keywords, explain what you are looking for and mentions your security clearance (if you have one). From what I have seen, ATS systems don't have a section for summary, but it does recognize it and pull out keywords that might relate to the job requirements. For this reason, we want to add our most powerful and impactful keywords and qualifications in the summary to slap the technical recruiter right in the face!

The email and contact information can come before, after or even be put into the summary. The ATS system will find your contact information, but for the sake of the human who will eventually review the resume, I usually label the Summary and keep the contacts up top just under my name.

For samples of ATS-style resumes check out:

convocourses.com/courses/resume

Here is what I put in one of my most recent summaries:

Summary:

> Prefer remote work. Twenty years of experience in cybersecurity implementing NIST 800 RMF with the public and private sector including interacting with federal government agencies such as the Department of Defense and NASA. Public Trust Level 6; DoD Secret security clearance (inactive), TS (inactive). Working on my AWS Certified Cloud Practitioner certification.

And a more effective way to list the summary would be to bulletize it. This will allow the humans who have to read it to absorb the information faster.

Summary:

- Prefer remote work
- 20 years of experience in cybersecurity
- NIST 800 RMF with the public and private sector

- Experience with federal government agencies such as the Department of Defense and NASA
- Public Trust Level 6; DoD Secret security clearance (inactive), TS (inactive)
- Working on my AWS Certified Cloud Practitioner certification

I put all the things that have the most impact and were the most important to me personally.

1. **Remote work.** I am telling them right away what I prefer. At the time, it was very important that I get remote work.
2. **Experience level.** I put all my years of experience. This is my most hard-hitting statement, because I know how important it is for the positions I am seeking.
3. **Keywords:** Keywords and phrases include "information system security," "NIST 800," "RMF," "Department of Defense," "DoD," "NASA." I know that ATS systems will pick up on these keywords.
4. **Security clearance:** Security clearance should have its own section, but since it doesn't, and I know it's something that some organizations look for, I put it right up top in the summary.
5. **Sneaky tactic:** The last sentence I put in is "working on" my AWS cloud certification. At the time of this writing, I don't have this certification. But by mentioning that I am working on it, I have now listed this keyword on my resume. I know that cloud technology is hot in my industry so I wanted to get it in there.

The summary should have your biggest strengths and best keywords condensed into how you can help the organization. You can use this same verbiage for your online profiles, which we will talk about later.

Keep the summary down to a few sentences. Don't write a novel. Get to the point. This section is optional, but you really want to use it to put in more keywords, sneak in your most hard-hitting assets, and your security clearance (if you have one).

Work Experience Section

List this section of your resume as "Work Experience" or "Experience." This is potentially the most important part of your resume and has the potential to get you a cybersecurity job the fastest because you list the most keywords, actions and impacts on the organization. This tells the story of your skills and what you can bring to the table.

Here is an example of an ATS-style work experience listed on a resume:

Work Experience

Verizon, Cybersecurity Analyst II, Herndon, VA – 09/2019 – 05/2022

- Performed cyber threat analysis using tools like Recorded Future for a private company whose assets were under attack by external threat actors; took the organization from having multiple breaches to having a low risk and earning a full security certification within a year.

For this section, ATS systems are looking for six things on your resume:

- Label "Work Experience" or "Experience"
- Work role
- Company you worked at
- Dates range you worked
- Location
- Bullets with keywords

We will go much deeper into what needs to go into this section of the resume when we dive into "Keywords in Work Experience".

Education Section

You need to put your highest level of relevant education on your resume. This means if you are looking for an entry-level position, that will require a GED or a high school diploma. If the job requires a bachelor's or master's degree or PhD, you will need to put this on your resume in the "Education" section.

The education section on an ATS format resume needs to have the following:

- Name of institution
- Degree
- School location
- Years attended

First, list the section as "Education." Then add the degree followed by the college, the location and year of graduation.

Here is the ATS format for the "Education" section of your resume:

Education

Associate Degree – Information Systems – Missouri University School of Business – 2017

- Completed an online course in cloud technology
- Extensive training using network scanners
- Earned a certificate in blockchain technology

*The extra bullets allow you to add more keywords. Here are more good examples of cybersecurity degrees listed.

- *Bachelor of Applied Sciences (B.A.Sc.), International Business, 2012, Illinois State University, Bloomington, IL*
- *George Washington University, 2000–2004*
  Bachelor of Arts, Information Technology
- *Bachelor of Engineering, Electrical Engineering, 2008*

Vanderbilt University, Nashville, TN

- *University of Rome, Italy, Bachelor's Degree, Applied Mathematics, 2001*

Even if you didn't get your degree but finished some college, you can still list what you did. It's still acceptable to include your college education if it's relevant to the job requirements. What you will do is list the number of credits obtained. For example:

University of Phoenix, Santa Fe, AZ
Computer Science, 55 Credit Hours Obtained

While we are on the topic of degrees, you should know that there are cybersecurity jobs that don't require a degree. Some entry-level positions are more focused on someone willing to get in and do the work.

Most high-paying cybersecurity jobs will require a degree. If you have some combination of high-level security clearance, specific experience or skills the organization needs or an IT certification that they require, then sometimes organizations will overlook the lack of a degree for these high-paying positions.

Acceptable degrees in cybersecurity

There is a misconception about the required degrees in cybersecurity roles. Many people think that you must have a degree specifically in cybersecurity to get a cybersecurity role. While there are positions that call for a very specific degree in cybersecurity, most will take any computer-related degree. This includes information technology, information system, information management, database, computer science, data analytics or any other degree with a direct connection to computers.

In fact, with some experience or technical skills in computers or if you can prove that you can do the work, many cybersecurity roles will take any science, technical, engineering, or mathematics (STEM) degree.

If all of this is discouraging you because you don't have a degree, or you have a degree in liberal arts, don't be discouraged about getting into cybersecurity. I have known a few cybersecurity badasses making crazy money with no degree. Two of my technical mentors (among the most gifted people whom I have ever met to this day) did not have a degree. And they would talk really bad about anyone who said they had one. My argument to them was that these days many companies are asking for an academic qualification and it's easier to find a good job if you have one.

One of my former coworkers had a master's degree in Egyptology (which I didn't even know was a thing). He worked with me doing NIST 800 security compliance. And another coworker could sing really well; turns out his degree was music or something. He was one of the smartest guys on the team. What all of these people had in common was that they had something that the organization wanted. Some skill. Some experience. Some certification.

Certifications Section

If you have IT certifications you should list them on your resume. Do not add expired or irrelevant certifications. For example, the CompTIA Security+ actually needs to be maintained with annual fees and continuing education. If these are not met, then the certification will expire. Once expired, don't add it to your resume. These certifications are very easy for employers to check so don't lie about it.

Do not add irrelevant certifications on your resume that is focused on a specific cybersecurity role. For example, if you are going for a cybersecurity analyst position at a security operation center (SOC) at a government agency, you should not add your certified nursing assistant certifications on the resume. But if you are going for an information manager job at a hospital, adding all of your health-care-related certifications and licenses will help you.

Here are how certifications should be added.

Certifications
CompTIA Security + Certification
Project Management Professional Certification (PMP)

List out the full name of the certification and if there is an acronym, add that as well. This does two things. It allows an application tracking system to pull the information provided into its database and match it to the known certifications that it has stored and it adds two keywords for job search engines.

In my experience, the hierarchy of resume highlights are experience, computer or STEM degree, and IT certifications related to the role. I have seen more people with experience and a certification get jobs than I have people with just a degree and no experience get a job. And in cybersecurity, even if they get in with no experience and a master's degree, their pay might suffer. Experience holds a lot of weight.

But don't sleep on certifications. Depending on the cert, it can be like steroids for your salary when you put it on your resume. The ISC2 CISSP, Certified Information Systems Security Professional, changed my life.

I am offered way more money; employers are constantly contacting me. I am asked to teach lower security certifications. And sometimes, employers don't even care if I have a degree because they see the CISSP and the skills they want.

But CISSP is not even the best cybersecurity certification!

The best certification is the one that most employers in your career path are asking for. That could be a Certified Ethical Hacker (CEH), CompTIA Security+, SANS GIAC Intrusion Analyst certification (GCIA) or any number of IT certs. It really depends on whatever the organization has a requirement for. And with the research you are going to do on keywords for your chosen career path, you will know what IT certifications are needed.

Check cybersecurity category certifications

Each category of cybersecurity has a specific set of certifications that are required or preferred or just helpful to landing roles within the specialty areas. Categories are described in the chapter on career paths and in much greater detail in book 2 of this series as well as the National Initiative for Cybersecurity Careers and Study (niccs.cisa.gov).

I am in the category of Oversee and Govern under the specialty area of Information System Security Manager (ISSM). In my experience, the top certifications are some of the following:

- CISSP
- CASP
- CISM
- CISA
- ISC2 CAP
- Security+

Penetration tester and ethical hackers are in the cybersecurity category of Oversee and Govern as well as Analyze. They have the specialty area of Network Services and Exploitation analysis. These specialty areas include certain certifications that hold more weight. Some of these certifications include (but are not limited to):

- OSCP

- GPEN
- CEH

Each category of cybersecurity has its own group of certifications that employers look for. Even if you don't have the preferred certifications, you can put on your resume that you are "Working on the CEH." You can put this in the summary of the resume so that anyone looking for a CEH, will see your resume pop up.

We will go into certifications, cybersecurity career paths and cybersecurity categories in greater detail in book 2. See appendix A for recommended entry-level certifications.

Skills Section

The "Skills" part of the resume is an excellent opportunity to add more keywords. This section is a great way to show skills that you did not put in the summary or work experience section. The skills section allows you to get straight to the point rather than trying to list every keyword in the experience section.

One thing to remember is that you are not just stuffing keywords here. If you cannot explain how you used the skill during a possible interview, then you should not list it. Consider this: if it is a skill they really need at their organization, they will ask you about it.

One time I mentioned "cloud" on my resume. At the time, my only experience with cloud was that I'd gotten a cloud-based system certified a few times. I did not have experience implementing or maintaining a cloud-based system. But since I mentioned it on my resume, the manager asked me about every aspect of cloud and cloud security for 15 minutes straight. He went from a complex technical question about Microsoft Azure versus Amazon AWS implementations to examining risks of cloud scans. And when I could not answer any of those questions, he asked general questions on the differences between PaaS versus SaaS. Finally, he gave up and said, "OK, you know what ... we will avoid the cloud-based questions. I don't want to waste your time or mine."

He said this because I could not answer many of those questions. I was saying things like, "Sir, I am not sure about that one. I have never actually implemented Azure or AWS." Or "I am not going to try to BS my way through that technical question. I don't know the answer." Or "My only experience with cloud was getting them an authorization to operate. I am familiar with the FedRAMP process, which focuses on cloud compliance."

This entire line of questioning was based on me mentioning cloud twice. My point is that you should only list skills that you can speak on in some way. Because if the organization really needs that skill, they will definitely ask about it.

How to list skills

You can list skills at the bottom or top of the resume. But I list them at the bottom of the resume. I do this because, the summary is where I need to put my best assets. Next, I usually put either work experience or education because education is short and work experience is a better way to sell your skills, in my opinion.

When I do this section, I focus on the most relevant hard skills for the job I am targeting in cybersecurity.

Here is a great way to group your skills together:

Skills

Programming: C+, HTML, Fortran, COBOL, ADA

Security Compliance: PCI/DSS, NIST 800, NIST CSF, SOX, HIPAA

Security Analysis: Network forensics, Tcpdump, Wireshark fundamentals, silk, traffic analysis tools, intrusion detection system, packet engineering

Network Engineering: Cisco configuration, Cisco backups, IOS troubleshooting, RIP, OSPF, NAT, DHCP configuration

In this example we are making it easy for recruiters to read, and for an ATS system to accept. We are grouping similar skills together. We are also using skills relevant to the job we are trying to get. If you want to target another job, you can create a separate resume and add different keywords that are relevant to that job.

You can categorize the skills by types of technology, levels of proficiency or even vendors. The most important thing is that they are relevant to the career you are interested in.

Here are more examples:

Skills

System Administration: Active Directory, SCCM management, account management

Security Control Implementation: manage event log, manage audit logs, MS Windows hardening, configuration management, change control, disaster recovery plan

Cybersecurity tools: Nessus scanner, Wireshark, Nmap expert, Qualys, network scan, vulnerability manager

Skills

Programming
C+
HTML
Fortran
COBOL
ADA
Security Compliance
PCI/DSS

Security clearance tip:

If you have a security clearance, the skills section is a great place to add it. The security clearance does not have its own section so we have to list it where we can. Make sure you put it on top in the summary, but here is an example of how you could list it in skills as well.

Skills:

Programming language: C+, HTML, Fortran, COBOL
Security clearance: Secret, TS/SCI, Public Trust

Choose a Career Path

Now that we know the proper format of the cybersecurity ATS resume we need to choose the keywords to put into our resume. But before we can drill down on the keywords for the resume, we need to know what career path to choose.

You can choose a career path, but sometimes a career path chooses you! What I mean is you may already be in a career. Maybe it is a career you don't like, or something you are bored with, or perhaps you don't even know that you are in a career. You will know your current career path based on where most of your experience is. You may be able to use your current career as leverage to get into a path you want. Even if you are a sanitation engineer and want to be in cybersecurity, there may be a way to use the current organization you are in to start doing IT, which will lead to cybersecurity, or (at the very least) you can use the income from your job to invest in your education in IT and cybersecurity.

From IT to cybersecurity

If you are already working in information technology, you probably already have cybersecurity experience. You just need to add all of the security-related experience to your resume. We will go through some of the things that you can put on your resume to reflect your cybersecurity experience in the "Keywords in Work Experience" chapter. But first you need to know about the different specializations and categories in cybersecurity.

Cyber Security Workforce categories

National Initiative for Cybersecurity Careers and Studies (NICCS) has a comprehensive breakdown of cybersecurity categories, specialty areas and work roles in the cybersecurity workforce. Their categorization is a good way to understand which direction you want to go in with IT and cybersecurity.

Categories include:

- **Securely Provision** – architect and design secure information systems. The specializations in this category are:
  - Risk management
  - Software development
  - System architecture
  - System development
  - Systems requirements planning
  - Technology R&D
  - Test & evaluation
- **Oversee and Govern** – manage and guide so the organization can effectively conduct cybersecurity. The Specialty Areas include:
  - Cybersecurity management
  - Executive cyber leadership
  - Legal advice
  - Program / project management and acquisition
  - Strategic planning and policy
  - Training
- **Protect and Detect** – identify, analyze threats to internal information systems and networks. There are only a few Specialty Areas in this category:
  - Cyber defense analysis
  - Cyber defense infrastructure support
  - Incident response
  - Vulnerability assessment and management
- **Collect and Operate** – gather cybersecurity information that may be used to develop intelligence. Collect and Operate has these specialties:

    - Collection operations
    - Cyber operational planning
    - Cyber operations
- **Investigate** – investigate security events or crimes related to information technology. Investigate has two Specialty Areas:
    - Cyber investigation (cybersecurity analyst)
    - Forensics
- **Operate and Maintain** – provide support, administration and maintenance to ensure effective and efficient information systems performance and security. Here are the specialties:
    - Customer services / technical support
    - Data admin
    - Network services
    - System admin
- **Analyze** – review and evaluate incoming cybersecurity information to determine its usefulness for intelligence. Analyze has the following Specialty Areas:
    - Exploit analysis
    - Threat analysis
    - Targets
    - All-source analysis

These cybersecurity workforce categories and specialty areas will be covered more in-depth in book 2 of this series. For now, what we need to know is that cybersecurity includes management, policy, administrative technical, analytical and many other types of positions. The main takeaway is that cybersecurity is very diverse and requires many different types of experience, knowledge and skills. It's not just hacking.

The popular cybersecurity skill sets of hacking, coding and cracking have been popularized in movies, television and social media but as you can see there are seven categories with dozens of specialized areas and hundreds of roles to perform these cybersecurity jobs.

In my experience, most of the work roles in the Oversee and Govern category do not require any hands-on technical skills. There are some categories dedicated to analysis with nothing but analytical jobs. The investigation category is where you find digital forensics (another popular cybersecurity area).

In order to figure out which category to pursue, look at three factors:

- Interest
- Skills
- Money

Interests

Your interest in the cybersecurity category is important because it will determine if you will stick with what you may need to learn and how quickly you pick up the skills necessary. Interests can also make the job you choose fun.

Skills

With the right skills you can get into the position you want more easily. If you have the skills, you need to put them on your resume with keywords. If you don't have the skills, you need to identify what skills, tools and experience you need to acquire so you can put them on your resume.

Money

Last but not least, "Show me the money!" You should consider the money. If the IT or cybersecurity category seems like a good fit but the money is not quite there, you need to think about the time and resources you are going to put in and whether or not it is worth your time. Now, you have to understand that most entry-level positions are not going to start off with a great income, so when you consider the money, think about the end goal. If the work roles that you are building toward will not end up close to the kind of income you want, you may need to consider something else.

From cook to IT professional services

He was five years into his career as a chef when he realized that most of them don't make much money.

They say, "follow your dreams" or "if you do what you love you never have to work again" or "follow your passion." Frank Johnson did this but he found out the hard way that his "passion" was not quite paying his bills.

He had a degree from the Cambridge School of Culinary Arts. He managed to earn a position as a chef in two of the top restaurants in Boston within three years. But his dream was to make his own menu, create his own meals.

The first time he'd done so was for his mother when he was 12 years old. He brought her a hot bowl of minestrone, with clams, dried cannellini, white wine, lima beans and some of his own special ingredients. He remembers the smile on her face when she asked him, "Franky, did you make this?"

That's when he knew he had a talent for taste. He was spectacular with the spoon.

He'd won third place in the Concord Chili Cook-Off at 16 years old and he had won his wife's heart with recipe he'd concocted from his soul. He had validation of his skills and he knew he wanted to share this talent with the world.

Against his father's advice, he'd enrolled in the school of culinary arts. At his first job at one of the top ten restaurants in Massachusetts, he realized almost immediately that being a chef felt more like a job than art. He wasn't creating and being innovative; he was memorizing recipes of someone else's dreams and creativity.

He knew what was missing. He knew what he had to do. But he needed a little help.

"Dad, hear me out." Frank put a hand on his old man's shoulders and gave him that sly handsome grin that he'd inherited. For a moment it was like looking into a future mirror. His old man was just an aged reflection of himself. "I know how you feel about my work and—"

"You mean cooking." Pops shook his head. "How's the pay? Is it as good as engineering?"

Frank nodded. "I know you wanted me to be an engineer like you. But—"

"Franky," his pop said, laughing, "you know you're like your mother. So stubborn. Son, just tell me how much you need."

"Dad, it's not like that. I wanted to tell you that you were right. Just hear me out." Frank squeezed his father's broad shoulders.

Frank Senior sighed. "I'm listening."

Frank looked out into a dream and used his hand to present an imaginary sign: "Franky's Italian Bistro."

His dad shook his head and nodded. "You want to start a restaurant?"

"Not just any restaurant, Dad." Frank smiled. "'Our' restaurant. A family restaurant."

Frank Senior was silent. He wanted to tell his son that being a chef and being a business owner were not the same thing. He wanted to break down the statistics of what happens to most businesses within 3 years and tell him about his own business that failed.

But instead, being a positive and encouraging parent, he signed a check.

Almost immediately, Frank junior realized that the restaurant business was not for him. He had to secure property, deal with banks, set up point-of-sale devices, choose designs and furniture, hire people. These things took him away from his passion. In fact, he eventually had to hire another person to be the chef!

Three years later, Frank Johnson was closing up the restaurant and enrolling in something he didn't particularly love but happened to be good at. Engineering. Software engineering, to be exact. He had a job at an IT company fixing computers before he even finished his degree in computer science. He made more in the first two years as a computer engineer than he did in five years of being a chef.

Frank still cooks, but he does it for his family.

I knew the actual cook who became an engineer

This is based on a true story. When I was working as a contractor for the army in the Middle East, we had to build a security information event manager (SIEM) from scratch on three different networks. The army had an agreement with the SIEM vendor. We needed their help on the first install and training on their product.

They sent three very sharp guys from professional services. I worked with them for about a week. We were on our way to lunch when I said to the team leader, "You're really good at this. You're writing scripts, setting up networks, configuring the system. How did you get into this?"

He smiled and said, "This wasn't my first choice. This is just a job for me. I was a chef for about five years."

I was shocked. That's when he told me about how being a chef made barely enough money to live.

"We cannot all be Anthony Bourdain or Gordon Ramsey, you know!" He laughed.

I could relate to this. Cybersecurity was not my first choice. I wanted to be a writer. My English teachers would often read what I wrote in front of the class. And this happened all the way to college. One of my teachers had a talent scout from Stanford interview me and check out my work when I was in high school. I submitted a dozen short stories to fiction magazines I read and got back-to-back rejection letters.

Looking back, I think there was nothing stopping me from continuing to write and try different genres, but by the time I became an adult I realized how much harder being a writer or an artist was than doing something like engineering. Besides, I was obsessed with computers.

I am not telling you to abandon your dreams. But what I learned was that it is a strategic move to get a job that makes good money to support your artistic goals and fantastic dreams.

After all, Frank didn't really cook for money as much as he just loved the joy it gave people to taste his delicious creations. And for me, writing is like a spiritual exercise. Making money with things I write is icing on the cake. Currently, I give too much of my content out for free to make a livable wage from it, so I have a job and writing is a hobby/side hustle until something goes viral. Hey, it could happen!

What to choose

Go through the categories listed. You can also do a search for "NICE Cyber Workforce" and check out the complete breakdown of all the special areas and job titles under each category. In book 2 of this series, we will deep dive into each Cybersecurity Workforce category and the requirements of each.

Choose something that makes a decent wage, something within your capacity to do and something you are comfortable with. For example, I did IT field support long enough to realize it did not make the kind of money I needed to support my lifestyle. I know my math skills are not good enough to do something like cryptography. And I am not yet comfortable as a manager. The jobs I have tried that worked for me are cybersecurity analysis, information system security officer and information system security engineering.

I have tried network engineering, customer support, programming and other positions that were really not for me, but helped to expand my knowledge and experience.

Tips for choosing the right career:

- Study the requirements necessary for a career
- Study the salary range of a career
- Study the industry of the career
- Try different jobs in a career path
- Talk to people already in the career path you want

Requirements of a career

Each career path has certain requirements at certain levels and categories within. If you become a help desk professional in the category of "Operate and Maintain" in the cyber workforce, one of the requirements will be the skill of troubleshooting workstations. The organization may have additional requirements such as certain IT certifications. In the role of a chief information officer, in the category of "Oversee and Govern," the requirement is different. The requirement might include 10 years of experience in a management role, a management degree and a background investigation.

Study the requirements of a career by looking at jobs in that career. Pay attention to the job descriptions, requirements and job preferences.

Salary range

Use search engines to see what the salary range of a career is. Look up job titles in the career path you are looking into. There are some pretty good sites that are out at the time of this writing. These include:

- Glassdoor
- Salary.com
- PayScale

Pay close attention to the average. The low and high parts of the pay are heavily affected by the locations, years of experience and the quality of the company. Some companies pay all their employees much higher than average companies. Facebook, Google, Apple, and Microsoft, for example, pay way higher. Another factor of pay to consider is the cost of living of the employees. Some organizations will pay you based on the cost of living of where you reside. Other factors that affect salary are security clearance and the level of responsibility. If the organization requires security clearances, sometimes they will pay a little higher than normal. Management, director or C-level positions will usually pay higher because there is more responsibility, stress, hours and pressure in those positions.

Study the industry

In the case of forensics in the "Investigation" category, studying the industry surrounding forensics will give you an idea of what is expected, who is hiring, what organizations have a need for forensics, and the types of people who get into this field. Watching videos from people in the industry you want to get into is very helpful. Pay NO attention to TV shows and movies that give a false impression of the job. If you watched the movie *Hackers* you would think that hacking was flying through a 1990s 3D rendering of "cyberspace." If you watched the movie *Swordfish*, you would think that all hackers look like Storm and Wolverine.

Hackers look more like Napoleon and Pedro.

If you want to see a realistic hacker movie, check out *The Girl with the Dragon Tattoo*, *War Games* and for TV shows check out *Mr. Robot* ...

Listen to people in the career path

One of the best ways to know whether or not any career path is for you is to listen to the good, the bad and ugly about the jobs in that space. If you want to be a pediatrician, listen to people who have been doing it for years. Listen to the men and women who love it and those who recently quit the profession. Listen to the horror stories of pediatricians. If you still want the career after that, then you are ready.

Use your job as leverage for the new career

If you are in a job right now and hope to expand into something else, you can use that job to get something you like. If you are getting paid, fund your path to another career. Fund your education by buying books and courses that teach you the skills and knowledge you need to start your new job. Pay for a degree, certification or license in the new field. This will take some work on your part, but if you really want the new path, you must stick with it.

Careers that can get you into IT

You can really go from any career field and transition into information technology if you want. I was a security guard in the air force and I cross-trained into computers. There are some career fields that are hungry for information technology professionals and cybersecurity people. Here are a few of them:

- Health care
- Law
- Financial sector
- Intelligence
- Government
- Critical infrastructures (pipeline, oil, gas, electric)

There are certain aspects of these career fields that might allow you to make a lateral move into IT or cybersecurity.

Health care – Health-care professionals have terminology and industry standards that most workers in this field have to know. For example, Health Insurance Portability and Accountability Act of 1996 (HIPAA) compliance and protection of patient information. There are actual IT professions that only exist in health care. Being a nurse, a Certified Nursing Assistant (CAN) or any other health-care professional can help you get a job in this field as an IT or cybersecurity professional at a medical institute if you get to know the basics of IT.

Law – When I transitioned from law enforcement to cybersecurity, I was surprised that there were many concepts that were relevant to both fields. For one thing the concepts of access control, assessments, privacy and logs are used extensively in law, law enforcement and security. As evidence has become more digitized, it has become more important to protect it as it goes through the legal system. Concepts like "chain of custody" make immediate sense to some in cybersecurity, particularly digital forensics. Forensics investigators are a part of law enforcement and investigations. It is also part of cybersecurity. If you are in law, physical security, investigations or the criminal justice system, you may be able to make a lateral change into IT or cybersecurity.

Financial sector – If you are in banking, investing, tax law, or funds management then you should know there is a big need for cybersecurity personnel who have some understanding of the financial sector. Deloitte, Ernst and Young, Price Waterhouse (PwC) and KPMG are known as the Big 4 because they are among the largest public accounting firms in the world (at the time of this writing) and they are constantly looking for risk assessors, auditors and cybersecurity workers. If you are a certified public accountant (CPA), a bank teller or in the financial space this will actually help you work in cybersecurity with these guys.

Intelligence & government – If you are in the military, military intel as an analyst or dealing with lots of classified data, you should already know there is a need for a professional who can protect all aspects of intelligence information. From cryptographers, cybersecurity analysts, mathematicians and programmers, all aspects of cybersecurity are needed to protect classified information.

Exercise: Top Five Choices

Step 1: Look at the NICE Cyber Workforce jobs

Look at each category to get an idea of which ones best fit you. Is the "Oversee and Govern" a better fit because you have a business degree and have been managing for years? Are you excited about getting into doing technical hands-on in the "Operate and Maintain" category?

> Go to this site for more details on each category: niccs.cisa.gov/workforce-development/nice-framework
>
> Or check out book 2 of this series.

Step 2: Choose a specialty area

You need to go through each category and check out each special area. Write down which ones appeal to you most.

Step 3: Select work areas

Drill down into each specialty area and take notes of the work areas that you would like to do, seem fun, or seem like a good fit.

Step 4: Brainstorm jobs

With just a pen and pad write down all the jobs you would like to do. Don't worry about what is good or bad for now because you are going to let the ideas flood the page.

Step 5: Circle the top 5

On your list of jobs, choose five that stand out. You will either have a "good feeling" about them or have some connection to them. Maybe you have experience with them and you're surprised that they are were part of the special areas. Perhaps you have a friend who did that job and you know it's great. Whatever the reason you can only choose five so choose wisely.

Step 6: Study your top 5

There are three things we are going to look at for your top five jobs:

- Look at the industry of each job
- Look at the salary range of each job
- Find videos of people who talk about these jobs

The search engine is your friend. But your best resource is if you know someone who is already doing this job.

Find Keywords

Stop!

Do not start this chapter without your list of five jobs!

You should have an idea of job titles, industry, and places to find more information on these jobs.

This list of five is important because we will find keywords based on these jobs.

Before we start the resume, we should gather keywords on each of the areas you have chosen.

Gather job titles

Take the job titles you have written down and use job search engines to analyze the keywords found in posted positions and resumes.

For example, let's say you wanted to get into forensics. First of all, your research should have given you an idea of some of the job titles in this career path. Just typing in your job into a job search will give you a few. This is the first thing you need to do, gather job titles. You must use a job search site in the top ten of the country you want to work in.

In the case of forensics, we type "forensics" into indeed.com and immediately we see autocompletion show the following:

- Forensic science
- Forensic science technician
- Forensic scientist
- Forensic social worker

But we are looking for computer forensics. We need to narrow our search. We can actually type in "computer forensics" or we can use the NICE Cyber Workforce as a reference guide.

On the NICE framework resource, you can do a search for your job title, but the best way is to identify the category, navigate each specialty area and look up "Work Roles." We will explore this in detail in book 2, but for now check out the NICE framework summary in this book to get an idea of each category.

Forensics is under the "Investigate" category, which has a specialty area called "Digital Forensics." The work roles under this specialty include cyber defense forensics analyst and law enforcement / counterintelligence forensics analyst. Using these key phrases from the NICE framework, we can gather additional job titles from our top job search sites and we come up with this:

- Host cyber forensics
- Network cyber forensics
- Cyber defense forensics analyst
- Cybersecurity analyst
- Cybersecurity engineer
- Security operations center analyst
- Cyber threat analyst

You will notice that not all job titles are obvious. They don't all have the word "forensics" in the job title, but have it as a required skill in the job description. You will find this in some jobs you go after. This is because organizations can name the job title whatever they want. There is no standard for naming jobs, which is why you have job titles like "Digital Overlord," "Retail Jedi," "Wizard of Light Bulb Moments."

Key requirements, qualifications, and responsibilities

Now that we have an idea of what job titles are in digital forensics, we can start looking for requirements that employers are looking for.

Use any of the top job search sites and go down the list of job titles. We are going to look up jobs that have been posted in the last month.

In this example we are using "Cyber defense forensics analyst" jobs posted on Indeed.com in the last 14 days.

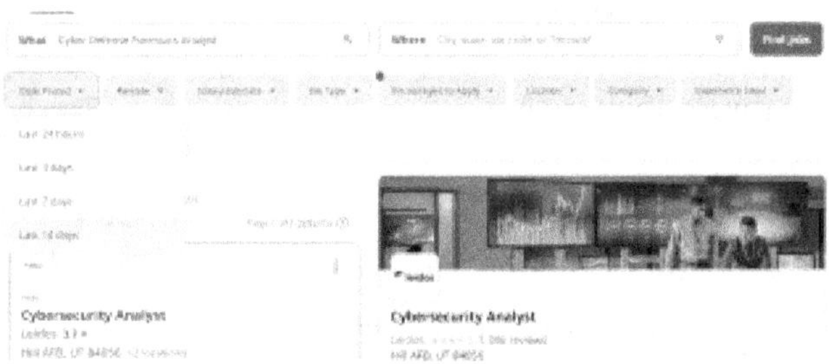

We will use multiple job titles from the list we gathered and we are looking at the last 30 days because we want the most current and accurate data from today's job market.

If you conduct this search and there are no results, choose another position title or expand the days.

We are looking for the requirements of the job to get an idea of what we should have on our resume and gather keywords.

Cyber Security Vulnerability Researcher, Forensic Analyst

KBR
Lexington Park, MD 20653
Full-time

Apply now

Required Qualifications:

EDUCATION

- Masters Degree in Cybersecurity, Computer Forensics or related field from an accredited college or university.

OR

TRAINING

- NEC 742A Network Security Vulnerability Technician
- NEC H10A Basic Cyber Analyst/Operator

OR

DOD 8570 CERTIFICATION

- Computer Hacking Forensic Investigator (CHFI)
- GIAC Reverse Engineering Malware (GREM)

AND

- 5 years of relevant experience:

OR

ON THE JOB TRAINING

- NAVEDTRA 43350 (Malware); with privileged access.
- NAVEDTRA 43469 Watchstation 303 Information Assurance Technician Level III

The very first results for our "Cyber defense forensics analyst" title say that the requirements include:

- a master's degree in cybersecurity or related field
- or training in network security vulnerability
- or a DoD 8570 certification
- or a computer hacking forensics investigator (CHFI)
- or GIAC Reverse Engineering Malware (GREM)

We need more keywords, so we will keep searching. The next job mentions "Basic Qualification" and "Responsibilities." I pulled data from five job requirements, responsibilities and qualifications to look for a pattern of what employers are looking for.

Using just "Cyber defense forensics analyst" as a search, I saw that many of the jobs are in the federal government, specifically the US Department of Defense. They are security operating centers. They are usually looking for someone who is eligible to obtain a security clearance or has one already. I noticed the wanted skills in host-based and network forensics, full packet capture, NetFlow. Another thing I noticed is that they wanted you to be knowledgeable in TCP/IP, IPS/IDS and SIEM tools.

The certifications they wanted included those mentioned on a document called DoD 8570. They mentioned Security+, CEH and GSEC to name a few. So, from here we would want to know what "8570" and each certification they mention is.

8570 refers to the Department of Defenses' list of approved IT certifications. Other federal organizations and contracting organizations have started to use this list to figure out what certifications a potential candidate should have. See Book 2 for more details.

Visual method of identifying keywords

Aside from just taking notes on the keywords as you find patterns in different jobs, another thing you can do is use word art. There are word art sites that allow you to upload words and get a visual representation that shows which words are used more.

Step 1. Copy the keywords from five job descriptions

Go to one of the top job aggregators and copy the primary responsibilities, requirements, basic qualifications, and preferred qualifications. You can copy then into MS Word, text, or Google Docs or whatever; you just need some way to copy them. You will need about five jobs, but if you can get more that works better as long as they are for the same type of job.

Step 2. Paste the job text into WordArt

Use WordArt.com or a site that is similar and paste the words you copied into the site.

For WordArt.com:

Click "Create"

Select "Import"

Paste the job text into the "Import words" message box

Click "Import words"

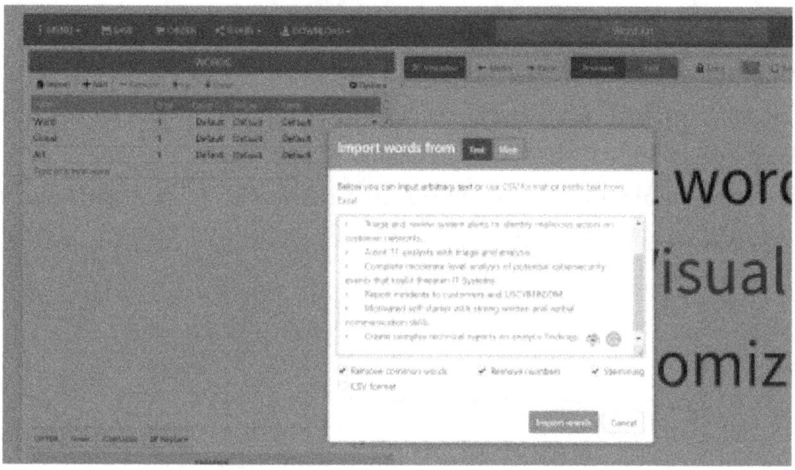

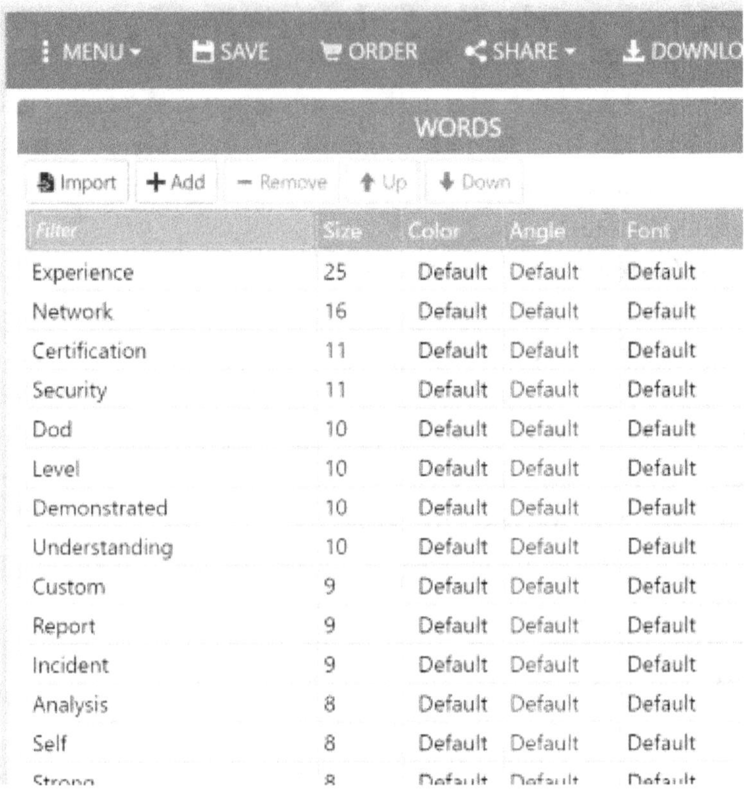

Filter	Size	Color	Angle	Font
Experience	25	Default	Default	Default
Network	16	Default	Default	Default
Certification	11	Default	Default	Default
Security	11	Default	Default	Default
Dod	10	Default	Default	Default
Level	10	Default	Default	Default
Demonstrated	10	Default	Default	Default
Understanding	10	Default	Default	Default
Custom	9	Default	Default	Default
Report	9	Default	Default	Default
Incident	9	Default	Default	Default
Analysis	8	Default	Default	Default
Self	8	Default	Default	Default

Once you import words, the app will extract all of the keywords and show how many times each word is used across all of the text you uploaded.

Step 3. Create the WordArt

Click "Visualize" to create a visual representation of the data you copied. The larger the words in the word art the more it is used.

In our example, the largest words are *experience*, *certification*, *security* and *network*. Other words that are used multiple times include *demonstrate*, *understand*, *report*, *incident* and *analysis*.

This gives us an idea of where to focus because what we can do from here is put all these repeated individual words in context. We need to dig into what "experience" do they mean across each job. What "certification" are they looking for? We can find out by looking at notes that we used to copy and paste. Within our visual representation we need to look for specific cybersecurity keywords that will enhance our resume. We can see a few here for digital forensics:

- Create report
- Packet
- TCP/IP
- Incident
- Capture
- OSI
- Protocols

Looking at other peoples' resumes

The next thing we want to do is look at resumes of other professionals who are in the field we are searching. You can find these on LinkedIn. Do the same search for the position and job title but this time look for "People" instead of "Jobs."

Pay close attention to the top 20 professionals. Look at their profiles and what are they saying in their "About" section, the places they worked, and their experiences.

Work experience is really important since this section will have the most keywords and key phrases. Not all professionals make this information public so you may need to look at multiple LinkedIn profiles until you find one that is public.

Once you find a profile that has its work experience public, pay close attention to the keywords they put in their work experience. Read what they did in the position and the software and hardware they used (if any).

You are looking for patterns. You can use the word art trick on their resumes to get an idea of where to focus your search for key phrases. You will need to use at least three resumes and/or jobs in word art to get a good number of keywords. But the more you use the better the results. All the resumes, profiles and jobs you use need to be relevant to the job you are targeting.

Copy the way these top professionals word their experience in their respective fields. I am not telling you to lie on your resume and copy word for word what they did in their job. I am telling you to word your own matching experience similar to theirs. You will need to paraphrase and use your own style but use the exact same keywords.

Look for patterns

As you are reading through job descriptions, requirements and resumes in a specific area, you are looking for patterns. Once you read enough of them, you will notice that the same five or six IT certifications are popping up. You will notice whether or not degrees are necessary, if they can be replaced with experience or what types of degrees are needed.

Certain knowledge and skills will be repeated. You want to find those patterns and make your resume have some of those patterns.

Keywords with little or no experience

I don't encourage lying on your resume. And I am not telling you to copy skills and experiences that you don't have. If you have no experience at all in the area you are trying to go in, then this exercise is going to give you a very good idea of what you need to build to. You can still start building your profile, but you will need to start studying the basics and creating home labs to engage the common body of knowledge in information technology.

See appendix A, for a breakdown of each entry-level certification that I recommend.

Keywords in Work Experience

Work experience is important enough to deserve its own chapter (twice). This is where we can put in the most keywords. Work experience is where the technical recruiters and employers will spend most of their time if you are even considered for a position.

As we discussed, work experience in the ATS format requires a job title first, then the company, then location (optional) and finally the time frame in the following format – XX/XXXX (month/year).

Each role that you performed should have its own section.

Instead of paragraphs describing what you did at the positions, you must use bullets. So instead of paragraphs like this:

> Performed a vulnerability scan using Nessus across the network. This was part of a quarterly assessment of vulnerabilities with the vulnerability management team. This also helped the compliance of a critical system.

You will use bullets like this:

- Performed Nessus vulnerability scan for quarterly assessment
- Assisted vulnerability management team during mandatory assessments
- An essential part of the system security compliance effort on a critical mission system

The bullets are easier to process. It breaks out all the tasks individually to highlight each thing that you have done. The next step is to add impact to the actions you put in bullet form. It will look like this:

- Performed Nessus vulnerability scans for quarterly assessment of 100 mission essential systems; created dozens of reports for the decision-makers
- Assisted vulnerability management team during mandatory assessments to mitigate thousands of system vulnerabilities

- Created documentation as an essential part of the system security compliance effort on a critical mission system; was able to attain approval to operate three times

Cybersecurity action and impact

In order to get the employers to hire you as a cybersecurity professional, you have to put your cybersecurity skills on the resume.

If you have no experience in IT at all, this section will give you an idea of what experience you will need to build going forward. If you have any IT experience at all then there is a good chance that you already have some cybersecurity experience and you need to list it on your resume.

You can find cybersecurity experience in implementation, maintenance, configuration and monitoring. Security controls are the security features that protect the information system. This means everything from controlling physical access to encrypting the data to privacy procedures.

For any security controls that you have had anything to do with, you will need to provide the action performed and the impact on the organization. There will be times when you only mention the action, but the impact will really sell the action, so you want to add it whenever you can.

In order to get cybersecurity positions, the work experience should reflect all the security work that was done in your previous positions.

CIS critical security controls and best security practices

If you are trying to get a cybersecurity position, you will need to put the work you did applying CIS controls. If you have little or no experience and what to get a security position, then take notes because these are some of the things you can do to get your foot in the door.

The CIS security controls are a great place to figure out what cybersecurity skills employers are looking for. There are many other security compliance frameworks and control families we can use, such as NIST 800 or ISO 27001, but CIS is good for this type of breakdown. Formerly known as SANS critical security controls (SANS Top 20), they are now called the CIS critical security controls.

If you have applied, configured, reviewed or had anything to do with the following security controls, you need to have it on your resume:

- CIS Control 1: Inventory and Control of Enterprise Assets[1]
- CIS Control 2: Inventory and Control of Software Assets[2]
- CIS Control 3: Data Protection[3]
- CIS Control 4: Secure Configuration of Enterprise Assets and Software[4]
- CIS Control 5: Account Management[5]
- CIS Control 6: Access Control Management[6]
- CIS Control 7: Continuous Vulnerability Management[7]
- CIS Control 8: Audit Log Management[8]
- CIS Control 9: Email and Web Browser Protections[9]

---

1. https://www.cisecurity.org/controls/inventory-and-control-of-enterprise-assets
2. https://www.cisecurity.org/controls/inventory-and-control-of-software-assets
3. https://www.cisecurity.org/controls/data-protection
4. https://www.cisecurity.org/controls/secure-configuration-of-enterprise-assets-and-software
5. https://www.cisecurity.org/controls/account-management
6. https://www.cisecurity.org/controls/access-control-management
7. https://www.cisecurity.org/controls/continuous-vulnerability-management
8. https://www.cisecurity.org/controls/audit-log-management

- CIS Control 10: Malware Defenses[10]
- CIS Control 11: Data Recovery[11]
- CIS Control 12: Network Infrastructure Management[12]
- CIS Control 13: Network Monitoring and Defense[13]
- CIS Control 14: Security Awareness and Skills Training[14]
- CIS Control 15: Service Provider Management[15]
- CIS Control 16: Application Software Security[16]
- CIS Control 17: Incident Response Management[17]
- CIS Control 18: Penetration Testing[18]

---

9. https://www.cisecurity.org/controls/email-and-web-browser-protections
10. https://www.cisecurity.org/controls/malware-defenses
11. https://www.cisecurity.org/controls/data-recovery
12. https://www.cisecurity.org/controls/network-infrastructure-management
13. https://www.cisecurity.org/controls/network-monitoring-and-defense
14. https://www.cisecurity.org/controls/security-awareness-and-skills-training
15. https://www.cisecurity.org/controls/service-provider-management
16. https://www.cisecurity.org/controls/application-software-security
17. https://www.cisecurity.org/controls/incident-response-management
18. https://www.cisecurity.org/controls/penetration-testing

CIS Control 01 & 02: Inventory and Control of Assets[1]

In these controls the organization documents and tracks all their systems. This includes the software and hardware on desktops, internetwork devices and anything with an IP address connected to the network. This is important because if the organization does not know what is on its network, then they don't really have a secure system.

If you have participated in the control of assets, you might say something like this on your resume:

Activities:

- Conducted periodic hardware/software inventory assessments; tracked 1,000 assets in large environment.
- Maintained inventory of all equipment, software, and licensing
- Created and maintained a software/hardware inventory, network diagrams and assessment documents; resulted in 2 consecutive authorizations to operate packages
- Created SCCM reports and fine-tune software/hardware inventory to get customized reports for various audit purposes
- Coordinated activities in the organization related to ordering, receiving, storing, and distributing IT materials and equipment; important assets are distributed on time
- Utilized DPAS database to maintain accurate records for all 1,000 assets and to facilitate inventory controls and reporting requirements
- Responsible for investigating discrepancies and inventory shortages; recover $25,000 worth of critical equipment
- Worked directly with management to provide updates on stock inflow and outflow for effective decision making
- Assisted in development of procedures to keep inventory records accurate

---

1. **https://www.cisecurity.org/controls/inventory-and-control-of-enterprise-assets**

CIS Control 03: Data[1] Protection

Data protection is about more than just encryption. A data management plan will address what data is being stored and for how long. As well as who will access it, where it is stored and why it needs to be protected.

Work on data protection might include the following:

- Configured data access control lists based on a user's role; ensured 500 users and every system have access to exactly what they need
- Established and maintained the data inventory in accordance with the organization's data management process
- Enforced data retention in accordance with FISMA compliance
- Encrypted data on 500 end-user devices using Windows BitLocker and Apple FileVault; these mitigated risks associated with end-user devices being stolen
- Encrypted data on 500 removable media to protect against inadvertent data loss
- Implemented Transport Layer Security (TLS) and Open Secure Shell (OpenSSH) to encrypt sensitive data in transit
- Deployed a data loss prevention (DLP) tool to identify all sensitive data stored, processed, or transmitted through enterprise assets

---

1. https://www.cisecurity.org/controls/inventory-and-control-of-enterprise-assets

CIS Control 04: Security Configuration of Enterprise Assets and Software

An organization must have control over their system's configurations. These are the security configurations of all assets and software.

If you have performed this security control then these might be the kinds of bullets that can help you:

- Established and maintained a secure configuration process for network infrastructure; the hardened 30 critical network devices include Cisco and Juniper devices
- Configured session locking on 210 servers and end-user systems; enabling session lockouts helped prevent unauthorized access to devices
- Implemented and managed host-based firewalls on over 700 mission essential systems
- Configured trusted DNS servers on enterprise assets; including configuring assets to use enterprise-controlled DNS servers and reputable externally accessible DNS servers
- Enforced automatic device lockout on mobile end-user devices
- Enforced remote wipe capability on over 2,000 portable end-user devices

CIS Control 05: Account Management

The organization needs to know who is logging in to their system and what credentials they have. If a person leaves the organization, they need to have a system that removes access to their user accounts. They also need to have a process that controls changes to the user's account. This is account management and it is a huge part of cybersecurity.

Here are the types of bullets you can use:

- Implemented strong password settings that are in line with CIS control best security practices
- Installed multifactor authentication (MFA) on a large enterprise with Linux and Windows systems
- Disabled dormant accounts to remove the likelihood of old accounts being exploited
- Created an account management policy that the organization uses to conduct account management on critical mission systems
- Restricted administrator privileges to dedicated administer accounts

CIS Control 06: Access Control Management

Access control means controlling logical access to information, systems, and objects in the environment. The organization must grant, refuse, and remove access in a standardized, timely, and repeatable way across an entire organization.

- Used active directory to enforce and maintain access control policies through the enterprise
- Granted and revoked access to enterprise assets for new hires, rights and changes to over 100 users
- Maintained role-based access controls on all 500 users in the organization
- Managed active directory for classified and unclassified environments with over 1,000 users and thousands of systems for 2 years

CIS Control 07: Continuous Vulnerability Management

Continuous vulnerability management has to do with vulnerability patching and checking. The continuous cycle is discovery of vulnerabilities, prioritization of vulnerabilities, resolution of vulnerabilities and repeating the process.

- Set up system-level alerting, including CVE detection on the enterprise for 100 critical systems
- Used the CVE program, Common Vulnerability Scoring System (CVSS), and organizations proprietary risk scoring methods to help manage and prioritize vulnerabilities
- Used Security Technical Implementation Guides (STIGs) and Security Content Automation Protocol (SCAP) Compliance Checker (SCC) to remediate the vulnerabilities on over 100 mission essential systems
- Applied knowledge of adversary tactics, techniques and procedures (TTPs), Cyber Kill Chain, Diamond Model for Intrusion Analysis, MITRE ATT&CK framework, CVSS, open-source intelligence (OSINT), or other relevant network defense and intelligence frameworks

CIS Control 08: Audit Log Management

Audit logs are gathered on servers, end-user systems, routers and other systems to detect, prevent and understand possible security incidents on the enterprise.

- Ensured that audit logs were enabled in a mixed mode environment that included Red Hat, Windows and MAC systems; allowed detection of over 100 threats against assets and improved cyber hygiene
- Configured audit log storage to make certain there was enough space for logs for mission-critical systems and retention of log history in compliance with organizations 4 terabyte requirements
- Conducted 100 hours of security audit log analysis to detect anomalies or abnormal events that might match adversary tactics, techniques and procedures (TTPs) in the MITRE ATT&CK framework
- Retained 30 terabytes of audit logs across enterprise assets to satisfy audit and compliance needs.
- Experience with Linux/Unix based Information System Security requirements to include archiving audit log data using port 514

CIS Control 09: Email and Web Browser Protections

Since email and web browsers are the main way internal users interact with external and internal systems, it's important that the organization have protections in place. This means educating users on social engineering attacks and having antivirus tools installed and updated.

- Created training for all 70 employees on the proper usage of Web browsers and web-based products
- Updated signatures on enterprise antivirus software for the proactive protection of 1,500 end-point devices and servers on the LAN
- Set up DLP technologies like Proofpoint Email, DLP & CASB, Microsoft Information Protection (MIP), Microsoft Security Suite (Defender, DLP for OneDrive, and others)
- Conducted threat intelligence using endpoint detection and email threat protection; a crucial part of the incident response process
- Used DNS filtering services for all enterprise assets to block known malicious domains
- Placed restrictions on unauthorized client extensions for Chrome, IE, Firefox and other browsers as well as email clients
- Implemented DMARC policies to reduce the number of spoofed domains
- Managed email filter on the enterprise to restrict the risky file types to improve the security posture of the organization security posture

CIS Control 10: Malware Defenses

Every enterprise in an organization needs to have antivirus that protects all systems. The system will not constantly update in virus definitions and antivirus software.

- Deployed and maintained antivirus solutions on the organizations systems; protected 1,500 systems across the enterprise
- Disabled autorun and autoplay on 1,500 end-user devices for an extra layer of protection against malware that might be on removable media
- Provided support of the anti-malware program, forwarded alerts and warnings to users; created tickets for potential security incidents involving malware
- Continuously monitored server and firewall logs, as well as network traffic, to check for security incidents and traces of possible malware
- Installed antivirus and malware detection on thousands of mission essential systems

CIS Control 11: Data Recovery

Data recovery means prioritizing the data that needs to be stored, protecting the stored data and having a plan to recover it.

- Established and maintained the data recovery process of the organization for all critical data
- Performed scheduled tape backups on systems as required. Manage data backup library to include storage of tapes for 15 legacy systems
- Performed system backups and recovery on 10 mission-critical systems
- Performed system backups to ensure expedient restoration of the database for the respective network equipment
- Performed system backups to ensure expedient restoration of the database for the respective network equipment

CIS Control 12: Network Infrastructure Management

Networks are made up of information systems that must be configured, installed updated and maintained. Security must be put in place for internal, DMZ and external network systems.

- Created network diagrams and documentation for NIST 800 security compliance and network infrastructure management
- Established a secure network architecture by maintaining address segmentation, least privilege, and availability
- Maintained centralized network authentication, authorization and auditing (AAA) using Cisco router using Radius and TACACS+ protocols
- Used secure network management and communication protocols such as 802.1X, WIFI Protected Access 2 (WPA2) Enterprise
- Documented and controlled all ports, protocols and services on three network enclaves
- Created wired and wireless network designs on new networks
- Conducted provisioning, installation, configuration, and troubleshooting for network devices

CIS Control 13: Network Monitoring and Defense

Networks will have congestions, human errors, vulnerabilities and cyberattacks on a regular basis. Especially if the network has critical systems, has access to the Internet or has lots of users.

- Provided cybersecurity analysis on network traffic for the enterprise using tools like security information and event management (SIEM) tools such as Splunk
- Deployed a host-based intrusion detection solution on 600 end-user devices and 14 servers
- Experience detecting host and network-based intrusions via intrusion detection technologies like Snort and Splunk
- Experience implementing protocol analyzers Antivirus (AV) and Host Based Intrusion Prevention (HIPS)
- Deployed a network intrusion detection solution on enterprise assets on a large 15,000 system enterprise. This included a Network Intrusion Detection System (NIDS)
- Performed traffic filtering between network segments

CIS Control 14: Security Awareness and Skill Training

In an organization the ignorant users are the weakest link. All users who have access to the enterprise need to have a level of training equal to their level of access. This includes security awareness and skills.

- Taught security awareness to 400 employees in the organization resulting in users clicking on 30 percent fewer suspicious links during phishing campaigns
- Created basic training on mission essential systems, which included skills and security training for 45 personnel
- Trained 55 workforce members to recognize social engineering techniques such as suspicious phishing attachments and links and questionable calls
- Educated operational users on proper authentication best practices. This included creating strong passwords, password storage and the importance of screen locking
- Created guidance on protection of personally identifiable information and the causes of unintentional data exposure
- Gave training on how to identify and report security incidents
- Conducted role-specific security awareness and skills training

CIS Control 15: Service Provider Management

Most organizations have service-level agreements with multiple partners, vendors and service providers. In many cases, they are also service providers themselves. These services include cybersecurity consulting, vendor maintenance contracts, cloud, network, and management services. The organization must monitor and organize all service providers associated with their main mission or business. This is done with policy, service-level agreements, contract and other legal documents.

- Constructed a service-level agreement (SLA) for support of the organizations mission-critical services
- Updated the organization's service provider management policy to include additional services and remove those no longer necessary
- Ensured service provider contracts for network devices (Cisco IOS and Juniper) included security requirements
- Included PCI and SOC2 [regulation or framework] compliance with providers during assessment of service providers

CIS Control 16: Application Software Security

If an organization develops applications, they need to implement them securely using the software development lifecycles (SDLC). Even with web application ... especially with web applications, the organization needs to implement best security practices to protect users, clients and employee data being handled by the apps.

- Provided application security during the application development process; included vulnerability management, security of third-party code and application security testing procedures
- Implemented security software development framework (SSDF) during the software development process
- Processed and addressed software vulnerabilities discovered in application using scanning tools such as Nessus and Web Inspect
- Performed root cause analysis on security vulnerabilities discovered on software; identified patterns in the development process that created the vulnerabilities
- Maintained an inventory of third-party software components and ensured that any updates to components that are used in any part of SDLC are still compliant with the overall policies
- Analyzed the security posture of the organization applications with a severity rating system to determine the risk to the organization
- Used standard hardening configuration templates for applications and associated components including servers, databases, components, cloud containers, platform as a service (PaaS) component, and software as a service (SaaS) components
- Separated mission-critical production and non-production systems; this separation allowed the organization to have non-production testing environments to identify and remove vulnerabilities before putting them into production

CIS Control 17: Incident Response Management

All systems eventually have some sort of incident that renders the data on the system harder to access, corrupt, and modified in a way that was not authorized. There are incidents that take out a network, server or device or even cause sensitive information to be stolen. These incidents can be caused by accidents, malicious intent (criminal hackers) or nature. The organization needs to have a plan to respond to these incidents and that is where incident response management comes in.

- Critical part of the incident handling team; responded to 15 incidents on mission essential systems
- Established and maintained contact information for reporting security incidents involving potential malware on the network
- Assigned a key role and responsibility in the incident response process for the organization; responding to 5 security incidents
- Conducted after-action reports for incident response exercises on mission essential systems

CIS Control 18: Penetration Testing

Penetration testing includes having a team attempt to exploit vulnerabilities in networks, web apps and systems.

- Conducted penetration tests internally and coordinated with third parties for 7 organization assessments
- Developed processes and procedures to incorporate findings into vulnerability management programs for 5 clients and the organization
- Conducted vulnerability assessment testing and penetration testing for 4 clients
- Performed penetration tests and vulnerability assessments using the approved DoD vulnerability scanners (ACAS), Defense Information systems Agency (DISA) Security Technical Implementation Guides (STIGs), Security Requirements Guides (SRGs) and other DoD software assurance security tools
- Used network analysis and penetration testing tools such as; Kali (BackTrack), Metasploit, Rapid 7 Nexpose, NMAP and Wireshark
- Conducted and document Security Test and Evaluation (ST&E) and physical security penetration tests on 5 mission systems

Create a Profile

At this point, you should have used relevant keywords for your targeted cybersecurity career path. You should have some of the CIS security controls and security best practices listed in your experience in action/impact bullets. One of the things you can do to make sure your cybersecurity ATS-style resume is solid is to run spell-check tools. You can also use a service like resumeworded.com or resumegenius.com that allows you to upload the resume so it can give you a quick free assessment. Make sure you run spell-check and proofread it start to finish.

Now that you have a solid cybersecurity resume, it's time to market it everywhere.

Before we start to market the resume, it is important that we gather all contact information that will be used on all the sites we are going to set up and the resumes we are going to make. This profile we are creating will act as notes. It will allow you to fill out the job site online profiles or give the cybersecurity job recruiters more information if they ask.

These notes are essential to every resume and online profile. It will help with privacy and organizing contacts once we turn on the marketing machine we will create.

Start with a blank page and add the following:

- First and last name
- Phone number
- Mailing address
- LinkedIn account (if any)
- Get a professional-looking photo of yourself – this will be used for online profiles on job sites
- Security clearances (if any)
- References (if any)

My profile example

Bruce Brown

□(719)

838-3799□□□□□□□□□□□□□□□□□□□□□□□□□□□□□□

contact@convocourses.com

https://www.linkedin.com/in/bruce-cissp-rmf/

Security Clearance:
Active Secret (1/1/2017)
Active Public Trust level 6 (10/2/2019)

References:
James Smith – 720-456-0565
Jimmy Johns – +1 217-356-9900
Samantha Billingsly – 1888-0987

Your name

I use an alias on my resumes and profiles. This is completely optional so feel free to skip this step and use your real name. But the reason I use an alias is that it is too easy to find your personally identifiable information using just your real name and city.

If you don't live in the USA, then this might not be a problem for you. Perhaps your situation is different. But in the US, you can type your real name and city in Google and it will have the last few places you lived, phone numbers, people you are related to and all kinds of other information you might not know is listed publicly.

Again, if you have a different situation feel free to skip this step and use your real name.

Contact information

For contact information, you will need to provide an email, phone number and location. Use an email that is best for you but keep in mind you may get hundreds of emails from possible employers. Whatever email account you use, also make sure you check the spam and junk folders often as some legitimate potential employers will get sent there.

You will get so many calls and texts that you may not want to use your real phone number. It can get very annoying. What I sometimes do is use a free phone number and have the calls go to voicemail but it's up to you.

The best resource for a free phone number is voice.google.com. With voice.google you can have all calls forwarded to your personal phone, voicemail or you can block calls and make it so they don't interrupt your personal life. Once we turn on the resume marketing, you will get enough calls to interrupt your personal life.

Security clearances

If you have any security clearances, you can add them here along with their status and when they were active. This is useful information for screeners, during interviews and for your online profiles.

References

You will want to write these down on your profile page. Don't post them on your resume or your online profiles, this is specifically for you. Usually if they ask about it, employers are looking to validate your experience at positions that you have put on your resume. So, you can send them the list of references separately.

For the privacy of the people you will list, you don't want to add these references to your resume because it will be uploaded publicly all over the Internet. Instead, on your resume, you can put something like:

> **References**
> *References provided on request

Make sure you inform anyone you are listing as a reference and let them know when the employer will call them if you know this information.

Resume scammers

I created my profile in such a way that it gives me an extra layer of privacy and protection, but there are some things you should be aware of to protect yourself further.

Lately, there have been scammers that will find your resume and attempt to scam you to get your banking information or even hack the company you currently work in.

There are some work-from-home scams that will have you stuffing envelopes after paying a fee. And you make a commission by signing other people up. There are reshipping scams that will have you receive packages to reship them to another place, but they don't send you a paycheck.

There are online jobs that have you assemble products. They have you pay for all the raw material and pay a fee but they reject the finished product.

Recently, there have been some fake job offers that almost immediately ask for your personal information. Once they get this, they can possibly steal your money or identity.

There are some red flags that will let you know this is probably a scam:

Fee or payment requirements. Most legitimate jobs ... correction, NO legitimate jobs I have ever had asked me to pay for anything. In fact, they will pay me for the pleasure of meeting me at the interview or pay my travel expenses if it is in another town. If someone is asking for a fee to even start their service do not do it. If you are starting your own business, yes. There are all kinds of startup costs, but for a job as an employee or contractor, no. There are no fees.

Download documents or files. There are some elaborate social engineering hacks that will have the criminal hacker pretend to be a technical recruiter, then have you downloaded malware. Do not click on any links or open any attachments anyone sends you. If they send you a document with the job description, scan it before downloading it. Do not download any files. If they send you a link, open a new browser and go to the site yourself. Or, better yet, go to the next potential job.

Early requests for sensitive information. It is not uncommon for employers to eventually get your social security number to conduct a background check. But normally, this is after you get an offer. This means you have been through more than one interview and talked to multiple people. And even then, you are entering your information into a secure site with an established background check organization. If they are asking for sensitive information too early, you should be suspicious. I have had technical recruiters ask me for my social security number the first time I talk to them. The answer is no.

The fake job offer that destroyed a multimillion-dollar organization

In 2021, a senior developer working for Sky Mavis applied for jobs. The company was OK to work for, but like all professionals, he was trying to level up and make more income.

Sky Mavis was doing very well. They'd developed a game called Axie Infinity. Axie Infinity was one of the first successful blockchain-based games that allowed players to make an income by playing. Avatars that gamers purchase to play have market value. In this game the avatars can be traded, bought and sold. Axie is like a Pokémon game where you can make money collecting, fighting and participating in the game! At one point the game had over 2 million active daily users and was making something like $15 million dollars per day. Some gamers were literally making a living with this "play to earn" model.

The senior software developer was approached by a company that encouraged them to apply for jobs on LinkedIn. They quickly had multiple rounds of interviews with increased difficulty.

After passing all the interviews, they were given a very generous offer. The offer was sent via a PDF.

The PDF was downloaded after signing up for the job offer. The company that did the interviews was actually a hacker group.

With the malware, the group was able to gain access to the Sky Mavis' network. The attackers went straight for the company's cryptocurrency wallet, which did not have adequate security. Sky Mavis lost $540 million dollars. This crippled the economy of Axie Infinity.

Further investigations revealed that the hacker group was associated with the North Korean government, which had successfully hacked another companies' cryptocurrency.

This is a cautionary tale for everyone in cybersecurity and IT. There are several ways that this could have been prevented. However, we won't go into how the organization did not have proper protection of their cryptocurrency infrastructure, or how there was very weak internal network security that should have caught this. We will just focus on what the job seeker can do to avoid this.

1. No downloads. Do not download anything from untrusted sources.
2. Scan downloads. If you feel you MUST download files from untrusted sources, scan anything you download and do not open it on a network with access to anything important (i.e., banking info, cryptocurrency wallets, sensitive information or corporate infrastructure).
3. Do not click random ass links. Do not click on links from untrusted sources sent via text, or email.
4. Scan links. If you have to click a link, you can check the link by copy/pasting it into a site like VirusTotal.com to check it for malware.
5. Too good. If the offer sounds too good to be true it probably is.
6. Conduct research on the company. Real companies will have a presence online and a number you can call to give you more information. Do not rush. Take your time to research the company. Find what employees have said about it. Find articles, press releases, and social media posts about the company.
7. Check the company's reputation. Check out the company's web page and see if the job is listed publicly. Sometimes they will have more information about the position and even the salary that they pay for it that they don't want to discuss in the interview.

In all my years of doing cybersecurity, getting hacked, seeing organizations get breached, conducting risk assessments, what I have learned is that anyone can "get it." That means anyone at any time can get scammed and victimized. No one, and I mean, no one, is exempt from getting scammed by clever attackers who have to take from you to gain anything. But for goodness sake, do not make it easy for them. Become a hard target.

Market the Resume

There is a passive and active side to marketing your resume. We are going to go through both of these.

Passive has two components: filling out the job site's profile and uploading your resume.

Actively market your resume has a few things you can do, but the main thing is applying for jobs.

Let's start with the passive side of marketing your resume.

Passive resume marketing

In this context, passive means you do something once and that work continues to bring results. In this case, the heavy lifting is done in your keyword research, resume building and filling out everything you need in the profile. If you have done your homework, then this will feel like a lot of copy and paste.

If you skipped all the keyword research and resume building, you will still need to do it.

Passive: online profiles and resume upload

Public Safety Announcement: If you created the profile in the last chapter, you will want to use that to help create the online profile. The last chapter was optional, but you have been warned. If you don't listen to what I am saying in this book, you only have yourself to blame when you get a million calls from all the call centers on earth. This shit works but you have to protect yourself, your privacy and your peace. OK. Let's get into this.

Most online profiles are about the same. They will ask for the same information and take about the same amount of time to do. Some of them can be filled out with your ATS-style resume and some are still manual. The more thorough you are with the online profile, the more attention it will get.

You will need to edit the online profile and fill out all sections with your resume information. Even if the job search site does this for you when you upload your ATS-style resume, you will still need to upload your image, add some skills, and find anything out that is not done automatically.

Set the resume you added to public. Most job sites allow you to set the resume to public or private.

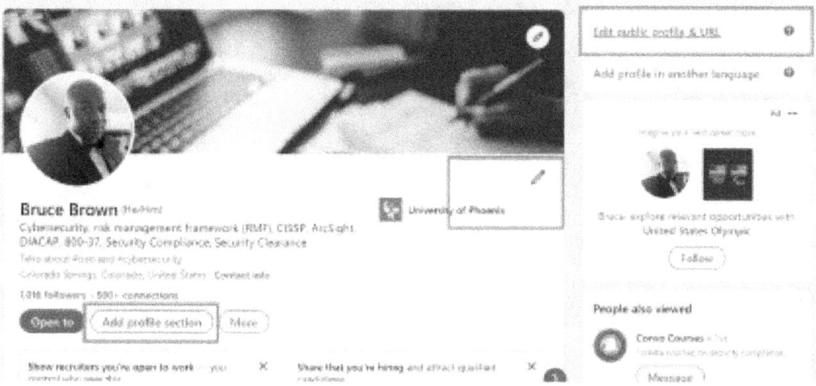

LinkedIn profile public

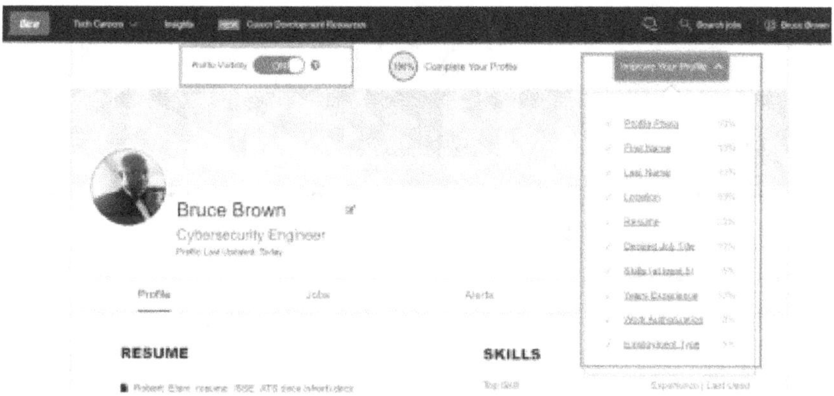

Dice profile public

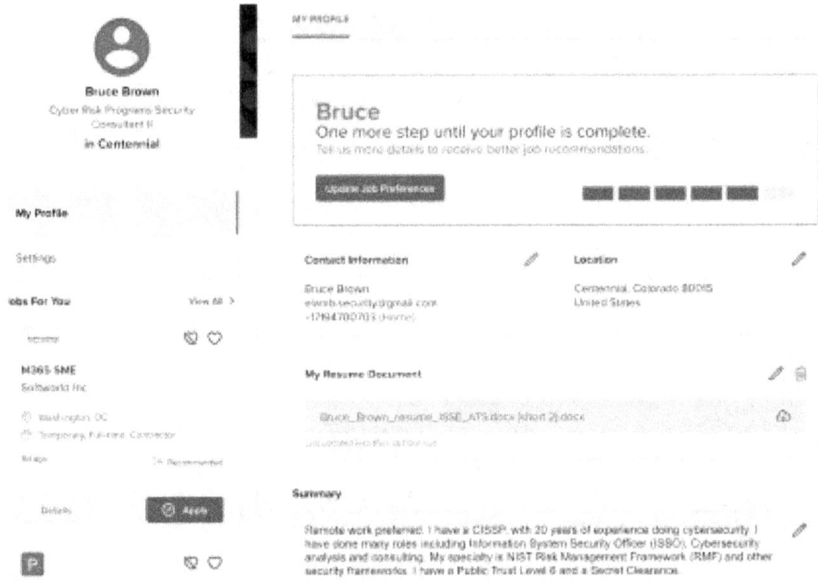

Monster profile edit

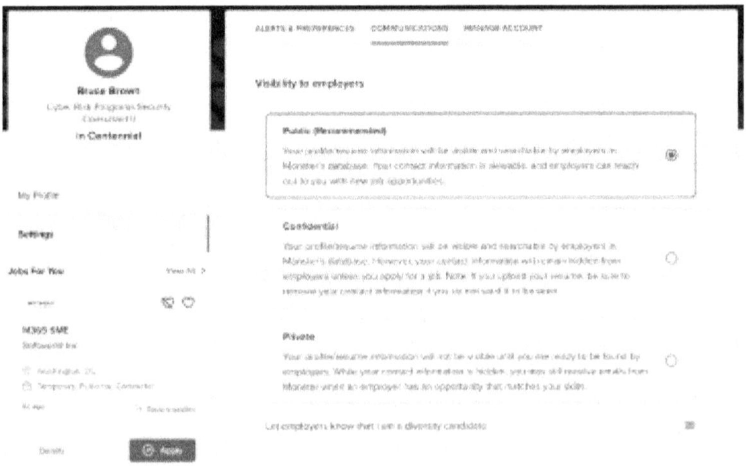

Monster profile public

All job search sites constantly change in style and usability. Links, features and buttons change but the most essential functions will be there. They will allow you to upload your resume, edit the profile to add more about yourself and allow you to make the resume public or private.

If you don't do these basic things, the job search will not be as effective. The online profile will usually give you an idea of what percentage of that you've completed. Get as close to 100 percent as possible.

Upload multiple resumes

You can also upload more than one resume to target different positions. For example, at one time I was a SIEM engineer and an ISSO. These are two different cybersecurity roles that have different certifications, experience and requirements. So, I create a resume for each.

Post your resume everywhere

You need to upload your resume to as many job search engines as possible. You never know which one will work for you. I get the most messages and interaction from LinkedIn, but most jobs I actually interview for are from Monster and Dice and every now and then I will get an incredible job offer from a random job aggregator that I forgot that I posted to.

Post jobs in at least the top 6 job aggregators sites. But the more you do the better your results will be.

Post your resume at the organizations in your industry

Find the organizations that are most dominant in your industry and apply for them. If your path is in the financial industry then you want to apply for the Big 4 account firms (Deloitte, PwC, KPMG, and Ernst and Young). You need to post your resume on their actual career sites. In the health-care industry, search for the top health-care companies.

At the time of this writing, the top health-care organization in the USA are:

- CVS Health Corporation
- UnitedHealth Group Incorporated
- McKesson Corporation
- AmerisourceBergen Corporation

All these companies need cybersecurity and IT professionals.

Your research will reveal where most of the jobs are for your cybersecurity category, specialty area or work role. For example, as an information system security officer (ISSO), I know that most of the jobs are in the federal government. What I do is search for the top government contract companies. Then I go to their career page and upload my resume.

Security clearance tips

There are job sites that specialize in government positions and jobs that require a security clearance. One great thing about these job site profiles is that they usually have a section for security clearances. If you have a security clearance, you will want to add it here. Here are some job sites that specialize in security clearance jobs.

- USAJobs.gov
- Clearancejobs.com
- Clearedcareers.com
- Silent professionals

There are many kinds of clearances but the ones you see most often in the USA are: Confidentiality, Secret and Top Secret clearances. You must be a US citizen to be eligible for these. There are positions of "public trust" but this is not considered a security clearance. So, although there is a background check, the candidate does not need to be a US citizen. Public trust background checks are often required for IT or financial positions supporting the government. They don't go as deep as clearances, but they do look at some of the following:

- Misconduct in employment
- Criminal conduct
- Deception or fraud in examination or appointment
- Refusal to furnish testimony as required for the investigation
- Alcohol abuse
- Illegal substances, without evidence of substantial rehabilitation
- Involvement with attempts to overthrow the US government by force

I am always asked, "how can I get a security clearance?"

First of all, a security clearance is not required for all cybersecurity jobs. The word "security" in security clearance is misleading. A security clearance allows an individual filling a specific position to have access to sensitive information. This can include positions like secretary, courier and many others.

If you want a clearance you have to get one directly from the government or from a contract. If you are a US citizen, some organizations will actually get you a security clearance if it is necessary for the job. These are obtained based on the needs of a contract with a governing organization.

For more on US clearances check out dcsa.mil

Passive: profile alerts and algorithms

Once your online profile is complete the site will do some of the work for you. The job site's algorithm will find jobs that match your resume then suggest jobs to you. They will also suggest your resume to employers. Some sites also allow you to set up email or SMS alerts that will notify you whenever a job matches your resume.

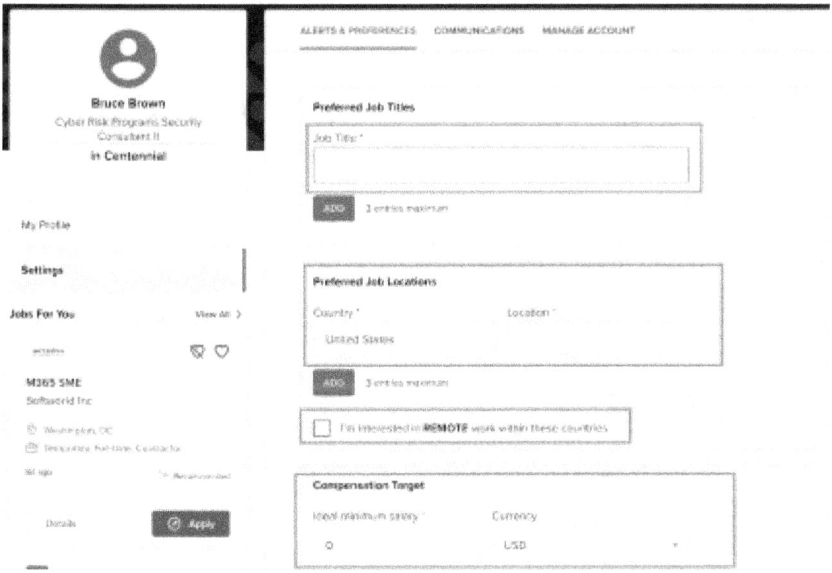

Active: applying for jobs

The active side of your campaign consists of applying for jobs on all the sites that you have profiles on. If you have filled out your profile completely, you will start getting pop-ups of jobs that fit your skills and experience.

You need to search for jobs using your keywords. You will see many jobs. But we need to filter the search to find the most relevant jobs. There are a few filters that you must apply on job sites. Here is how it looks on LinkedIn:

- Filter by jobs
- Search for jobs that are within the last month or two weeks
- Choose "Easy Apply"
- Search "Experience Level"

LinkedIn job search filters

On Dice.com you will do the same thing. Use your keywords to search for jobs, filter by a date range so it will only show recent jobs posted and choose "Easy Apply."

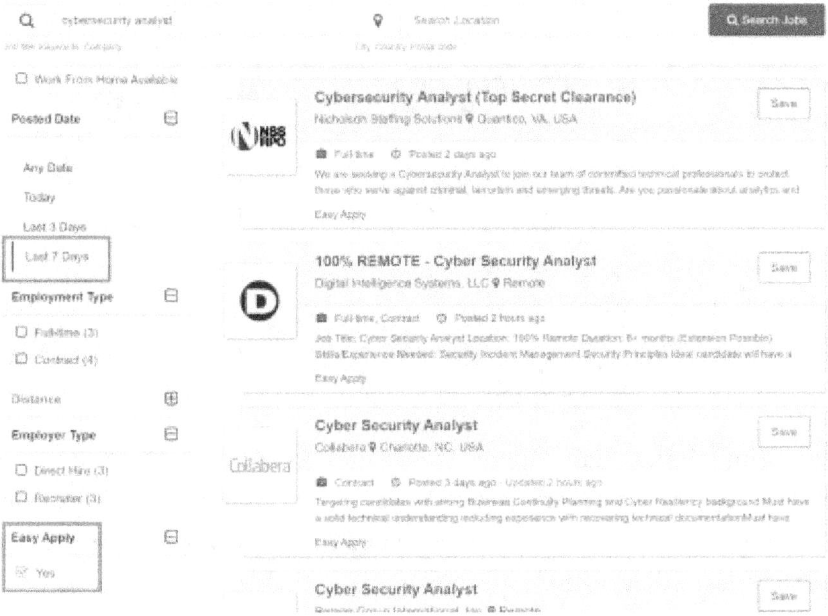

Dice filter

On moster.com, there is the same kind of filter for your job search.

Monster.com also has a “Quick Apply” feature.

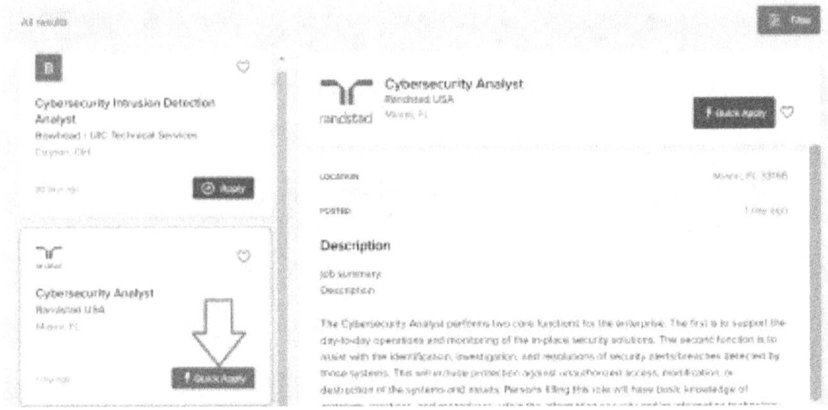

"Quick Apply" and "Easy Apply" features allow you to apply with just a few clicks because it pulls in data from your complete online profile. But the profile needs to be filled out properly and you need to upload your ATS-style resume. Many job sites will have this type of feature.

Conclusion: You Will Get a Lot of Messages and Calls

If you have taken action by doing deep keyword research, updating your ATS-style resume and doing passive and active marketing then you will get some contacts, opportunities and maybe even some job offers.

Results will vary. So much relies on your experience and skills in IT and cybersecurity. But even if you have no experience, this guide can serve as a map to plan where you want to go in your career. For example, if you know that you want to do digital forensics then your research will tell you what you need to do. You will need to study for it. But now you have a blueprint for you what you need and what the employers want.

Appendix A: Entry Level Certs

If you have ZERO IT experience you need to gain the skills and knowledge that can get you into an entry-level IT position. Going to University or community college is a great way to start. But there are pros and cons.

The pros of going to college are that some schools offer the skills and IT certifications in their degree programs; a degree is one of the best things you can have on a resume (for IT and cybersecurity jobs you will want to get a degree in STEM – science, technology, engineering, or mathematics).

The cons of going for a degree are that it can be expensive, it's very slow, colleges rarely teach exactly what you will be doing on the job (most of the good stuff you'll learn on your own).

Aside from pursuing a degree, there are some entry-level certifications that will get your foot in the door. IT certifications are actually supposed to validate the skills you already have, but the curriculum is so good on certifications that you can use it to build your knowledge and skills as you study for the tests.

There are many entry-level IT certifications out there. But there are a few entry-level certifications I would recommend based on their marketability, salary range and what they teach.

At the time of this writing, Comptia.org, Amazon and Google have the hottest entry-level certifications.

You can start with entry-level IT certifications. Here are a few that I would recommend you start with.

- Google IT Support Professional
- CompTIA +ITF
- CompTIA A+
- AWS

Google IT Support Professional

The Google IT certificates do not require relevant experience. At the time of this writing, there are two Google IT certificates available: introductory IT Support Certificate and an advanced-level IT Automation with Python certificate.

IT courses included in the IT Support program are:

- Technical Support Fundamentals
- The Bits and Bytes of Computer Networking
- Operating Systems and You: Becoming a Power User
- System Administration and IT – Infrastructure Services
- IT Security: Defense Against the Digital Dark Arts

Courses in the IT Automation with Python curriculum include:

- Crash Course on Python
- Using Python to Interact with the Operating System
- Introduction to Git and GitHub
- Troubleshooting and Debugging Techniques
- Configuration Management and the Cloud
- Automating Real-World Tasks with Python

Both courses are on Coursera.com for a monthly subscription of $39 USD (at the time of this writing).

This IT certificate is still pretty new compared to the other entry-level certifications. While there are some jobs that only require these Google support certificates, there are not many. Set up an alert on the job search sites to capture these jobs as they are posted.

As of 2019 the median annual wage for this certification was about $55,000. The salary will vary based on other certifications, any experience and location of the job.

If you really want to level up in your IT or cybersecurity career, eventually you will need to really consider some sort of degree program.

CompTIA Certifications

The CompTIA A+ certification was the first IT certification that I earned. The first certification will probably be your hardest because you're nervous and you have to get used to the types of questions. CompTIA certification, particularly the A+ and Security+, are very well known in every industry. CompTIA has four areas of certifications:

- Core
- Infrastructure
- Cybersecurity
- Data and analytics
- Professional

I recommend you stick with core if you have no experience and don't know much about IT. These are all entry-level certs that can get you on the path to getting your first IT position. The top entry-level CompTIA certs are:

- A+
- Security+
- Network+

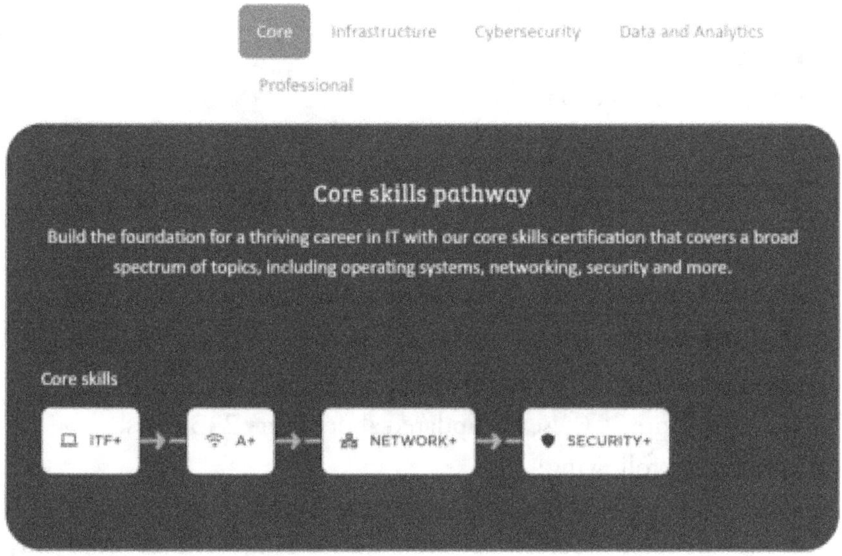

I would recommend the CompTIA A+. It will build your knowledge base of how information technology works. But if you feel like it might be too much, there is another certification that is more of an introduction. It's called the CompTIA ITF+.

CompTIA ITF+

Information Technology Fundamentals+ (ITF+) allows you to get familiar with basic IT knowledge and skills. It is for students preparing to enter the IT workforce and professionals changing to IT or IT-related fields. This certification is great if you don't even know if you want to get into IT yet. A+ certifications are a much larger commitment. The test is more expensive in time spent studying and money. ITF+ is specifically designed as a pre-career certification because it focuses on a broader understanding of IT for nontechnical professionals. It covers the following areas:

- IT concepts & terminology
- Infrastructure
- Applications & software
- Software development
- Database fundamentals
- Security

The test consists of 75 multiple-choice questions.

CompTIA A+

The CompTIA A+ consists of two separate certifications, Core 1 and Core 2. These are updated about every 2–3 years. A+ covers the following:

- A+ Core1 – mobile devices, networking technology, hardware, virtualization and cloud computing
- A+ Core 2 – operating systems, security, software and operational procedures

Both exams are 90 questions and multiple choice. Candidates must complete both exams to attain the A+ certification. According to payscale.com, the average CompTIA A+ holder has an average base salary of $66,000/year. But you have to factor in other things such as no experience, degrees and other certifications to get a more accurate view of the salary.

This also depends on the title, company and location. If you are getting the A+ certification as your first certification with no experience, your main goal is to gather experience so you can level up later. It is one of the most popular entry-level IT certs in the current market.

From the A+ cert, I would recommend going straight into Network+ or Security+ or both.

CompTIA Network+

I took this certification after I took the A+. Although it is not as marketable, it helps me to have a better understanding of networking concepts and the associated technology. Another good thing about the Network+, is that it is not vendor specific like other network certifications (i.e., Cisco & Juniper).

Network+ covers the following areas:

- Network fundamentals
- Network implementation
- Network operations
- Network security
- Network troubleshooting

CompTIA Security+

Security+ is one of the top 10 security certifications you can get in the industry. It is highly marketable. Because it covers so many requirements on the DoD 8140 approved certification list, it is on many contract job requirements.

Security+ covers:

- Attacks, threats and vulnerabilities
- Architecture and design
- Implementation
- Operations and incident response
- Governance, risk and compliance

There are 90 multiple choice and performance-based questions.

AWS Certified Cloud Practitioner

Cloud is a super-hot subject in IT and cybersecurity right now. Just having this certification will get your resume looked at. This certification is intended for anyone who has basic knowledge of the Amazon AWS platform. They expect you to have six months of exposure to the AWS cloud, basic understanding of IT services and their uses in a cloud platform as well as knowledge of core AWS services and use cases, billing and pricing models, security concepts and how cloud impacts business. For this reason, you should probably go for the A+ certification, network+ and maybe server+ first.

This is a 65-question multiple choice test.

www.ingramcontent.com/pod-product-compliance
Lightning Source LLC
LaVergne TN
LVHW022110200926
848481LV00003B/1135